Sub Rosa

Susan Prospere

W·W·Norton & Company

NEW YORK · LONDON

Sub Rosa

Susan Prospere

W·W·Norton & Company

NEW YORK · LONDON

Sub Rosa

POEMS

PS
3566
.R687
S8
1992

Copyright © 1992 by Susan Prospere

24141640

All rights reserved
Printed in the United States of America
First Edition
The text of this book is composed in 10.5 on 14 Bulmer,
with the display set in Facade Condensed.
Composition by PennSet, Inc.
Manufacturing by The Courier Companies, Inc.
Book design by Antonina Krass.

2 Sept. 92

Library of Congress Cataloging-in-Publication Data
Prospere, Susan.
Sub Rosa / Susan Prospere.
p.   cm.
I. Title.
PS3566.R687S8   1992
811'.54—dc20   91–25096

ISBN 0-393-03095-4
W.W. Norton & Company, Inc., 500 Fifth Avenue, New York, N.Y. 10110
W.W. Norton & Company Ltd., 10 Coptic Street, London WC1A 1PU

1 2 3 4 5 6 7 8 9 0

For my mother and father and brothers—
and for the one who loves me . . .

Forbid all Joy, & from her childhood shall the little female
Spread nets in every secret path.

—William Blake

CONTENTS

I

I I

III IN PETTO

I V

ACKNOWLEDGMENTS

Grateful acknowledgment is made to the following magazines in which poems in this collection have previously appeared:

The American Scholar:
"Ode to the Lightning Bug"

Antaeus:
"Passion"
"Peonies"
"Star of Wonder"
"Sub Rosa"

Field:
"Despair"
"House of Straw"
"Saturnalia"
"Tree of Knowledge"

The Nation:
"Heavenly Bodies" (as "Stargazing")
"Sophronia and the Wild Turkey"

The New Yorker:
"The Company We Keep"
"Farm Life"
"Frozen Charlottes"
"Heart of the Matter" (as "Into the Open")
"Milliner"
"Moving Pictures"
"Party Per Pale"
"The Pool of Tears"
"Silver Thaw"
"Ultramundane Traveler"

Poetry:
"Affinities"
"Ministering Angels"
"Oxford, on an Ancient Crossroads Beside the Thames"

The Antaeus Anthology, edited by Daniel Halpern
"Sub Rosa"
"Passion"

Mississippi Writers: Reflections of Childhood and Youth,
Volume III: Poetry, edited by Dorothy Abbott
"Silver Thaw"
"Farm Life"
"Star of Wonder"
"Sub Rosa"
"Passion"

The Best American Poetry, 1991, edited by Mark Strand
"Heart of the Matter" (as "Into the Open")

I am grateful to the Ingram Merrill Foundation for a fellowship that helped me in completing this book.

Love and thanks to Michelle Boisseau, Peter Cooley, Nancy Eimers, Richard Lyons, Gary Myers, William Olsen, and Charles Siebert. And special thanks to Jeffrey Greene, an abiding presence.

I

PASSION

For a dime in the 1930s my father bought a drawstring sack
                                              of chinas and cloudies
and knelt on the ground where a house had burned
to play marbles in the evenings with his brother and first cousins,
forming a circle inside the space marked on the property
by a cistern, a chimney, and gallica roses.
In the dusk he fired shots that sent his opponents into purgatory.

He taught us what he could of courage and the science of the earth:
of litmus paper turned pink by the juice of a lemon
or blue when dipped in water and bicarbonate of soda,
of mercury that scatters and convenes in a shivery dollop,
and the power of a gyroscope balanced on a string, wheeling
                                              down the airways.

What he didn't teach us is the mystery that holds a man
                                              and woman together,
my brothers and I each with marriages dissolving.
The time my brother crawled under the house to fix the plumbing
in the wet darkness, he carried a pinup lamp shaded with roses.
I think he was drawn by something provocative that we haven't
    discovered,
the electrical current from the lamp charging through his body
until he cried out to register the pain
of that terrifying moment when the voltage lit up his life.

SILVER THAW

How cold the angels are—
so they come down to Mississippi,
their breath rising from the ice of their bodies
to frost the clover.

And they take the trees one by one
because they are jealous.
All night we listen from the screened porch
as the trees ice over and break,
their branches cannonading as the angels load them
with their terrible artillery.

My mother plays old records of Big Band music
and we begin to dance—
my father, my mother, my brothers, and I.
We are embarrassed
because we move together without grace,
but say it is exercise, after all, to warm our bodies.

We say tomorrow there will be firewood,
divinely prepared, throughout the forest.
It is only a matter of taking the flatbed trailer
and filling it with these offerings.
We discuss the blessed nature of destruction
although we don't believe it.
The angels are famous for their propaganda.

When Yankee soldiers camped in Christ Church
three miles down the road,
they played lewd airs and dances on the organ.
The angels must have heard them
and left this part of the earth.
The growing seasons are long now
and stretch into winter.

In June there will be sweetheart roses
along the whitewashed fences.
Years ago I saw my father pin one on my mother
as if it were a corsage she would wear
to enter the evening.
Her body was limber then,
and the angels would have envied her had they seen her,
dancing in the Bahia grass a private dance
that did not include my father
or any of us who watched from an upstairs window.
This was the province of the sacred,
and we begged her with rising voices to come indoors.

STAR OF WONDER

My mother lights the pilot light
                    that guides us from one Christmas to another—

to the drumstick and the cat stealing milk from the creamer,
     the India rubber ball and the Tiny Tears doll
                              rocking in the cradle.
What mechanism in our heads makes us lie back,
                    open our eyes, and cry real tears?

Put
      away
            the toys;
                    we are grown now.
The sheriff's star my brother wore
                         to keep law and order in childhood
hangs between Styrofoam angels
       on a tree we fell at nighttime.

Pass the sherry, please, around the green tin trailer
                                   we haul the tree in.
Here's to sugarplum visions while my father has his eyesight.

Here's to a smile and a penny whistle, here's to a promise,
     to stars blown through the sky with peashooters at bedtime.

Crossing our paths, here's to the deer
                         captivated by our flashlights.

Good night.

We sleep in cigar box beds with four posts made of clothespins.
   Good night,
        good night to pickup sticks and good night to my father
                placing smoke capsules in the Lionel steam engine.

He is taller than the train we leave on.

   All aboard All aboard
                    we go faster
                                faster
past the plastic houses and the bristle trees
                    into the darkness under the wing chair.

FARM LIFE

Our contract with this world is not complete.
The natural objects seem reticent,
the dogwood hesitates up and down the ridge
to open its skim-milk blossoms.
It is afraid of our disapproval,
or that we will be merely obtuse
in not seeing its analogies,
the petals rusted as if nailed shut all winter.
They are wallflowers,
so I assure them again that they are invited.

We will do so much for money.
My father allows the lumber company
to come in for selective cutting.
The trees hide behind each other
because they have nothing to gain by standing
on tiptoe, the graceful ones,
or at attention, those that are serious
and make efforts at subservience.
They only end up in other people's woodboxes.
I can promise them nothing.

Only the machines rest easy in the shed.
They know they will clear the fields adequately
and will turn chaos into saleable bundles.
This is farm life, where we work
at cross-purposes with what was intended.
The monolithic bodies of the cows turn shy

as we move across the grass toward them.
Ahead of us they mingle with the trees.
The calves unfold from their mothers' wombs
in the equivalent dark of the forest.

Once we cut a hole too large in the nipple
of a bottle and drowned a calf with nourishment.
My father and I are complicitous on this earth,
though there are things we don't speak of:
the way he stacks his pennies in regular columns
and places his shoes by the bed
as if he stood over himself while sleeping.
He knows the mimosa leaves will close
if he touches them with his hands,
that the earth as yet is reluctant to receive him.

HEAVENLY BODIES

1

How the visiting schoolchildren must have
trembled in their adolescence
when Hilda Doolittle led them into the peerless room
of the Flower Observatory near Philadelphia
to gaze through the telescope
at the flat plain of stars.
They knew then that angels were frail
and pedestrian,
and carrying this revelation home,
opened *The Book of Knowledge*
to the "Things to Make and Things to Do" section
and constructed telescopes in their backyards.

2

In New Orleans a street peddler sold
glances through his telescope
outside Café du Monde, and in the swank hours,
people in evening clothes would fish
for dimes in their pockets
to look up at the moon caught in the sky
like café au lait inside a cup,
and when I looked, I saw,
for so little money,
that no one would ask me
to dance the two-step
under the artificial stars of the Blue Room.

3

My father taught me that the universe could move
in the ell of the dining room.
Turning an orange between his thumb and forefinger
before a light bulb, he made night fall
on the far side of the orange
where people slept in rice paper houses
after the Winding River banquets.
The shadows of the planets bobbed
on the walls of our house.
He was in charge of the Heavenly Bodies,
coming up the walk in midsummer to focus the sun
with a magnifying glass on a matchbook
until it flared through the centers of our lives.

Not much in my life has gone the way I wanted,
and I believe that we go a long time
under the earth without seeing.
My father's cataracts float
in formalin in the medicine cabinet,
though he can name the states in geographical order
and the constellations,
by picturing them in the darkness of his head.
He tells us that when he dies,
he will come in his pickup to drive us
to Emerald Mound
where the Big Dipper hangs over the oaks
and resurrection fern
like the tin cup we drank from at the cistern
the summer my mother lost her diamond
in the garden in a row of Kentucky Wonders.

HOUSE OF STRAW

Then the wasp returns to the vespiary,
the brown recluse carries its violin into the dark cupboard,
and the ladybug crawls down in the woodpile
                among the red hearts of the cedar. . . .

Is this an ending, or do you believe in Life Everlasting?

I remember we were transferred to New Orleans,
my mother crying at the supper table
while the red and green roosters strutted across the kitchen wallpaper—
out the window, disappearing, the homemade go-cart
with a hood of green linoleum, and the turtle with a shell
                painted with a Florida palm tree.

Can you take your home with you?

The summer it flooded, the fire ants formed balls
                to roll themselves across the water.
People slept on cots at Our Lady of the Sea School
and the river rose so high on the levee
the ships sailed on the current of leaves over the Garden District.
At night we slept below sea level under the rudder.

Do you believe that life is directionless?

There was dusting powder swirling through the hallways,
                the dark stain on my panties, a wand of mascara. . . .

Are you saying the answer lies within us?

I read *The Password to Larkspur Lane*, lying on the horsehair sofa.
Look, I said to my brothers, I'm holding the key to the world.
Then I curled the lid backwards, and we lifted the sardines,
                lying in rows, and smeared them on saltine crackers.
We ate them on the balcony while the poinsettias rotted below.

        Would you say this was the beginning of sadness?

My brothers threw a baseball in the evenings in their bedroom—
the light outside, the color of Four Roses poured into glasses—
until one night they threw it through the wall.
They covered the hole with a map of the world,
                and for years they kept it a secret,
the darkness spiraling, unknown to our parents, under Louisiana.

    What did they teach you about the scope of the world?

They said if we took our shovels in the backyard,
                we could dig a hole so deep we'd get to China.

        Is home a place you ever get to?

I remember the little holes the ant lions live in
                and the way they grasped the straws we lowered
as we chanted doodlebug, doodlebug, come out, come out,
                                your house is on fire.

ULTRAMUNDANE TRAVELER

Because you were the youngest, we told you
          you were adopted. Though you looked
     just like us, you could never see it,
your view of the world, slightly dyslexic;
          your face askew under the felt beanie
                    with plastic gyres and a turtle
          on a spring; your grasp, left-handed.
You thought you were amorphous, orphaned, negligible.

No wonder then, walking down Mars Road one evening,
          you hoped something vanguard and aluminum
                    might land in the arrowleaf clover
     to take you apart, and you would see us
                    reduced from afar,
sitting without you at the wrought iron table,
          spirit lamps low-lighting the party. . . .

The road will open before you, Orfeo,
          a voice spoke from the sky
     to Orfeo Angelucci, driving home from Lockheed
          after the nighshift,
     balls of green fire hovering in the air
     above him, and when he stopped,
he drank from the crystal cup placed on the fender
     for him. Inducted into mystery,
          he said he was refreshed as never before,
and when he returned to the everyday world,
          he said it was an abode of shadows.

You, too, believed in the pure light of invasion,
        that in your lifetime peaceable creatures
            would come to lift you
bodily into beauty, and you would ride
        on the simple ship of the 1950s
        drawn on wide-ruled paper
    with a thick pencil in your bedroom.
You put away *McGuffey's Reader* with tales
            of Hugh Toil and Mr. Idle
    to read how worlds collide. Outside
    the sheer curtains at your window,
                the ringed planets,
wide-wheeling, traveled through the skies.

We stand over you now at Baylor Hospital,
            charcoal pumping through your nose.
    For you, the cessation of desire
    made a world you couldn't live in. Next door
            in Imaging, they photograph the body
        under its skin,
    its shape more corporeal than we imagined,
        the ghostly bones and outlines of organs
            hanging in rows
        on fluorescent boxes. *Speak to him,*
the nurse says, and we call to you, each in turn,
        though I'm afraid you've traveled
    too far already to hear us,
                the instruments beside your bed,
the ventilator and the sphygmomanometer,
                monitoring you as you go.

Orfeo Angelucci slept once for a week,
                    and when he waked, he said
        he had been taken in a shining bubble
            with vortices of flame
                    for propellors
to a planetoid with nectar and ambrosia. Reclining
        in a shimmering chair,
                    he said he shocked the cosmic company
    with his erotic feelings for Lyra. Will you
                come back to search for mortal beauty,
or will we find you someday lying in the backseat
    of a car with a vacuum cleaner hose,
or breathing in the ethylene gas that issues forth
                    from the wounded tree-of-heaven?

SUB ROSA

In the distillation process, what can be
extracted from subterranean waters
makes a slight list: my mother, the depetaling
of a rose, and boarding houses.
In Tennessee even the darkness is a gradient
the insects climb, so when we grow tired, we rent rooms
at Red Boiling Springs for a whole season.
We say we have a suite for the summer
because the passage from room to room
takes us past the robins
as they flop against the earth,
having all day drained the chinaberries
of their spirits.
A boarder in the room next door has carved a mandolin
of an opulence we can't endure—
my brothers and I are only children.
While we are sleeping, the adults go down
to the healing waters to recover their losses.

My father drives my mother into 1934,
the stars fizzing over the top
of the open convertible as they head towards
the Peabody Hotel in Memphis.
They are dancing on the hotel roof
the night of their engagement,
chrysanthemums in pink and silver foil
lining the floor around them,
while the music of Buddy Rogers widens

like the Mississippi River towards Mary Pickford.
She has come tonight to join him,
her purse blooming
with tissues of blotted lipstick.
The small pressure of my father's hand upon her back
leads my mother into marriage.
They move together slowly, as the ducks,
gathered in from the fountains in the lobby,
rise on elevators to the hotel roof,
where they have flown loose into the present.

They settle on our pond as dusk
diffuses into the flowers.
Confederate roses grow redder in darkness;
all of us are older.
I watch my mother and father from the lawn
as they move into the kitchen,
though the light has made a double exposure,
casting the reflection of the garden on the glass.
They appear to settle their chairs,
not in the kitchen, but in the arbor,
the trees of papershell pecans enclosing them.
My mother, reaching into what she believes
to be the cupboard, will find it empty,
her hand drawing back from the bluebird house
suspended from the barbed wire fences.
In the bowl of his spoon, my father holds a rose
though he will not lift it.
The hour of secret consumption is over.
When darkness dissolves the reflection from the window,
I see them as I imagine they will appear
in the firmament—slightly abstracted,
caught, as they are, on the other side of glass.

PARTY PER PALE

Skinny-dipping in the kidney-shaped pool,
            sodium lamps lighting the highway
                  passing by us,
we synchronize our bodies, one stroke,
            two, faster, slower,
      through the dark, denatured water,
            breast stroke, butterfly,
      a crawl across the deep into the shallows . . .
as if we were together in amniotic fluid,
                  born in love,
      like the twin calves my father's cow
                  dropped in the pasture—
the female, a freemartin, blonde,
                  the loveliest I'd seen, sterile. . . .

Some nights she comes to me still,
                  dream-calf, velvet, cream
            on her tongue from her mother's udder,
      brushing past the beauty-berries
                  out of the bayou,
            the clink of her bell
                  like ice clicking in glasses
            held by the guests
at my parents' parties. Beyond the hedgerows
      I watched their shadows thrown
      against the windows—an ombres chinioses,
                  as they lifted their highballs
            to toast a birthday

or danced the grapevine twist
across the carpet. I believed in marriage then—
that after each party, love reconstituted itself,
the lipsticked glasses, the charred panatelas,
a lost earring,
assembling into couples
pairing off in low-slung cars,
tail fins flashing down the driveway.

Come back, my mother says,
anytime, standing in the doorway.
So long, so long, they call,
growing small, smaller,
waving down the driveway. So long
to Rayburn's Rhapsody warming the kitchen,
to sweet milk turning
in a milk glass pitcher,
so long to the calf the color
of honey. Of milk, curd, butter,
dung, and urine, she gave us only waste
and beauty. My father shipped her
somewhere he wouldn't tell us
though my brothers played out the scene
over and over,
linking the cars together
on their 00 gauge railroad—
the locomotive, the coal tender, the stock car—
the plastic cattle huddled
behind the lattice, unloaded
at way stations, whistle-stops, crossings,
until they were lost
in a romeo slipper or cardboard boxes

in the back of a closet. Years later,
rummaging through the attic,
my mother found one,
holding it in her palm, hardly remembering
how happiness was composed. *I swan*,
she said, looking across the rafters—
as if astonishment were a bird
heading out over open water,
its wings spread wide, uplifted.

II

MILLINER

It is only when the hour
becomes pained
with dusk
that you become
a visionary,
and you are able
to hurt us all
with your bits
of beauty—
the little chapeaus
in ovals,
the vine
of fox grape
twisted in a parabola
around the brim,
or the cherry
so red
we hold it forever
at the tongue's tip.

Ah! That wild
gladiola is a picture
of the fandango
you danced,
or here, a little cloud—

you must have worn
toe shoes
on each finger
to make such a bright
ballet of hat!

ODE TO THE
LIGHTNING BUG

By dark, when everyone dreams
of losing his clothes,
when Amy drops her blouse
over the rosebushes,
the lightning bugs open their topcoats
to fly, and their hearts,
enamored with the night,
light small temptations
in the minds of children,

who, in turn, move erratically
over lawns,
clasping captured lightning bugs
in their cupped hands,
until the night is filled
with the lit cathedrals
of the children's hands.

And Amy, luminous
in her own light, remarks
on these luciferin lanterns,
wonders aloud
if all plans are haphazard . . .

because all of us
imagine connections in our heads,
joining together these pinpoints of light,

dot by dot,
as we name constellations,
the dots of these bawdy figures
forming and reforming into schooners,
a three-ringed circus, lighted cities.

True king of summer,
fraudulent in its power,
each flash of light,
a laugh up its sleeve,
called *firefly* in tales of elegance
where paths are lighted
by their phosphorescence,

we know them here
as *lightning bug*, mixing
with a company of stars
until they confuse our senses,
our minds tired with sorting out,
forming perceptions
that change with each shift
in distance,
each flash of light,

though for the lightning bug,
even death is glorious
and predetermined,
whether collected in jars,
or smeared on sidewalks
by children into the names of children
where they flare up momentarily
in a final iridescence.

SATURNALIA

Peep Show

On a winter evening, the children have made
peep shows in shoeboxes,
each world meant to be microcosmic,
though even the light,
coming through the square they have cut
in the lid, is distorted.
We are drawn, as always,
to the outrageous, the man in a shiny suit—
cut unwittingly large by one of the children—
standing taller than the cotton smoke
drifting off the chimney,
than the fir tree in the forefront, glistening.

Procession

The hilarity after embarrassment.
The embarrassment, the kind of shyness
a magician's subject feels when made to appear.
Though these were ordinary children,
found in the open, and in the clearing,
the empty house near them was made
of cypress planks, notched together, nailless,
and the garlic had gone to seed around the cistern.
When the children plucked the purple clusters,
the odor taught them
that they had come this far.

There were the dogs that led them here,
charging through the orchard, barking.
There were the sounds that informed the dark,
the stars seeking out their relative positions.
There was the buck that ran faster
than the dogs, faster than the stars,
faster than the children.
There were the children who followed
with the attitude of those bearing musical instruments,
the rasp of kazoos, the miniature accordion.
The posture was the posture of a parade
because the children were anonymous.
This, though, was their sadness:
that the buck disappeared in the pin oak and pine,
the Spanish moss blurring his traces,
that the bark worn from the trees
showed them his passage,
the velvet rubbed from his horns
so that he might grow, in time,
the brow antlers, the bay, and the royal.

Pageant

Tonight the horses flare along the fences.
All day they have eaten the pears
fermenting in the orchard,
so that now in the darkness, there is only
the sheen of their haunches
and the feeble light
given off by fruit expiring.

The children leap from the hayloft
with coat hanger wings left over
from an Easter pageant
though the gauze fails to lift them
out of this sequence.
In the reaches of a lantern,
a blue runner spirits its way through the grasses,
thrilling the children,
though each of these creatures,
apart from the others, is harmless.
The snake, alarming in its closeness,
will seek cover along a wash in the loess,
the horses will be stabled,
and where one child has lain dizzy
in the straw,
an angel suggests itself the next morning.

SOPHRONIA AND
THE WILD TURKEY

We keep no chickens: my mother fears
that they will fly against the windows
the way they fly against the windshields of cars
that graze the highway shoulder.
So there is no need for a rooster—
the dark rainbowed feathers of oil on water—
or time, its announcement cleared
from the throat of a rooster. . . .

Then Sophronia comes walking down the road
from her house to ours, sometimes
one way, sometimes the other,
past the japonicas with a turkey that follows
her from the wild,
and my grandmother is alive for the occasion,
the two of them sitting under the morning glories,
open like a showroom of Victrolas.
Dance, Tom Turkey, dance,
and the turkey struts in the dust
while the rocking chairs sail onward,
and my grandfather is killed in an explosion,
rocketing into the universe ahead of his time,
and my father tells my mother
that the wild turkey is a stupid bird,
the chicks drowning in the rainfall
from looking upward,
and that Sophronia will be happy all her days

in a house papered with Sunday papers,
where the Katzenjammer kids have at it,
and someone on the wall by the stove
smiles as he offers her a Lucky Strike.

TREE OF KNOWLEDGE

1

Remnants of primary school—
saber-toothed tigers,
the horse's evolution, an isthmus or two,
and in complete sentences,
answers to the questions
about the Malayans'
way to make a living,
spear and fish,
and how little dressed they were.

In secondary school,
something of the body and the mind.
A frog dissected
so you realize you have lungs, too.
A simple tool,
a specimen slit open,
and the thin gray bulb
for breathing is not breathing.

And then the mind.
Geometric figures because the mind
is structured.
Slate and chalk, false and true.

2

The night the Institute burned
down past my bedtime,
they said *spontaneous combustion*:
old newspapers and rags
flaring into fire engine shine and ladders
and what I heard
down dream after dream after
were tiny fists hammering the brass dish bell
into alarum, alarum,
and the chuzzle and swish of the striking hoses
and what I saw
were periodic charts and charts
to show the phylum of the animal kingdom
go up in smoke
and all the heyday ranting
of children in the schoolyard
to burn the building down
became our burden.

Then the pinecone turkeys and the Pilgrims
from the Thanksgiving projects
descended into flame
and the scrapbooks burned
with the cellophane-covered,
pressed leaves of autumn.

MINISTERING ANGELS

When I saw the pony in June, she was dressed
for a different climate—something nearer
her ancestral beginnings (she was Welsh)—
for she had rounded the great climacteric turn
that left her hormones delicately imbalanced
and her eyes were misted over
as if the Atlantic Ocean had raised its tide
over the Welsh coast until it took her.
She would drink from the porcelain bathtub
in the pasture long drafts of invisible water,
then would stand for hours in the kudzu,
enveloped in its dark contagion,
while the horseflies drilled,
until they were dizzy, after her.

All one day I worked to remove the coat
she no longer discarded in the ardent weather.
I sheared her, lacking shears, with scissors,
operating them with blistered fingers
until they moved automatically, flashing
over her body like bright, clacking stars.
The tufts of hair falling around her
accumulated into a dark, furred shadow
that repeated her strange predicament
and would stay on the ground to remind us,
when she left, of the way
we collapse downward before rising.

So I willed her alive,
at least for one more evening,
the ministering angels walking all night
beside her through the orchard,
explaining the lie of the next strata,
while occasionally pulling down for her,
from the trees, the phosphorescent pears.
Before morning, having earned their rest honestly
through good works, they draw a bath
in the outdoor tub and bathe in the open,
relishing the high, post-Victorian moment,
having stayed on earth long enough to remember.

LOSS OF MEMORY

Bridging the gap
  between elm & ash: only the little bittern
    on wing from the branch
  of one multifarious tree
   to another. No more than drift
 on the shores of the waters,
    embued by Odin
   & his brothers with breath,
  comely hue & utterance,
    Embla & Ask rose from the void,
    took form, incarnate,
 to become the world's original lovers. But Odin,
   unconcerned, turned & walked
    the wavering way of the rainbow
  from earth to heaven,
    leaving them behind,
   once ash, once elm,
     forgotten.

    At the end of the rainbow
  from the left & right
   shoulders of Odin, two
  ravens fly off each morning,
    gliding over the earth,
   over ash & elm,
   over tremolite & tundra—
 one called Thought, one Memory—
   & peering through the gloaming,

Odin fears for the return
       of Thought, but even more, he says,
    for Memory. Blacker than Night,
   blacker than Darkling, darker
          than Space, they pass
    sometimes for nothing. Often it is Memory
       who loses the way,
          or stops—slowed
       by the weight of snow
             on its wings or the hostile
   currents—& for a while, drifts down
          into a warmer country,
       to the home of the Osage orange,
          its female tree fruitful,
             proferring. . . .

   Lingering below in earthly groves,
             girdled in light
          & bound in shadow, what gets lost
    along the way is nostalgia. Far
          north against the iceblink,
       the World Tree spreads
             its gargantuan branches,
          the Three Virgins of manifold wisdom
             rising from its shade
       to lay down the fates
          of the world's children—& Odin
       hangs himself from a limb
          with a spear in his side
          nine days & nine nights
             in the name of wisdom,
       sacrificing himself to himself—
             not to another.

III

IN PETTO

TUNNEL OF LOVE

O June bug harnessed by a thread,
   the mourning cloak lowering
     its proboscis to the Dubonnet bush
  to siphon a last drop, and Little Thumb,
asleep in the half shell of a walnut

in a blue violet bed with a rose petal
   counterpane. Over and over under the earth
     she sang in treble for the mole,
  Ladybird, ladybird, fly away home,
until the mole wanted to hold her forever

under the earth's surface. Each step darker
   than the other, they set forth together
     to wander through the winding tunnel,
  the mole holding rotting wood in his mouth
for a lantern, its phosphor dimmer

than the smallest hope she had ever
   turned to. Love can come this way,
     misshapen and exploratory, and love
  can fail, the imagination unable
to turn the blind and blundering

into beauty. For the mole, in the unfolding
                    of the story, there will be no end
                              to a grave and unshapely longing
          as he shovels through soil to make
each slow and difficult passage,

for Little Thumb left the mole and the linen
                    trousseau four spiders wove for her
                              on a wire form, no larger than a thimble,
          to fly over the melting countries
on the back of a swallow, her sash

interlaced through the sinuous vane
                    of his feathers. Behold the blue
                              and abiding waters and the marble
          palace with flowers growing wild
through a crumbling pillar. A tiny king

emerges, so pure of vision we can hardly
                    see him. Because light things align
                              with one another, Little Thumb married
          the spirit of the flowers, having fallen
without stopping through the endless

distance of his transparent body. Here's
                    to love made manifest, its essence
                              floral and unfurling, and here's
          to Little Thumb at her wedding
during *de lyse noetter*, the light,

faint but unfailing. The lords and ladies
          of the flowers gave her fly wings
                    for a present, so that she, in joy,
          could rise and lower from tubular
blossoms. Is this the passage

we long for into heaven, or does
          Little Thumb, sleeping by the pistil
                    and stamen of a flower, dream sometimes
          in sorrow of the slow progress
of the mole and his dark burrow?

HEART OF THE MATTER

How forlorn and lost
they must have looked, the mahogany deer
carved on the cabinet,
peering forth from the trailing
vines and foliage, antlers
intertwined, their bodies forever
suspended, frozen
as if jacklighted, as if having come
so far to the edge
of the forest,
they couldn't bear to enter
the room, with its stale air,
the claw-footed sofa. Coaxed
from the wood, whittled,
these fallow deer, clustered
around the keyhole, guardians
of some mortal secret. . . .

It was a woman's hand, I think,
that turned the key
to lock away some token, hidden perhaps
in her underclothes, lying under
her corset, its hooks
and eyes open. I like to believe
it was she, needing
consequence, image, passion,
who placed the china figurines
in the curio cabinet, almost touching,

the shepherdess and the sweep,
vivified, at least for a moment,
by closeness. Once they were slip
in a single bowl, poured
into molds of equal measure,
and set on the topmost
shelf together—she with a rose
pinned to her bosom, a gilded crook
beside her, but no sheep walk
to cross, no flock to tend to,
and he in pitch black clothes,
holding ladder and broom,
his face glowing,
having swept, as yet, no nooks,
no hearth, no ingles.

Day after day, lifted up, dusted,
placed on the shelf closer
and closer, the shadow of one
sometimes falling across the other,
they felt the shape
that love can take—the form of one
lying darkly upon the other—
and though you might say
they were only dolls, their features
glazed, their bodies rigid,
they, too, are of the earth, and I,
for one, have come to believe
in the primal sadness
of a divided substance. Oh, come

to me now, toting your ladder,
 and we'll go, as they once did,
    past the opening night
   at the doll's theater,
past the one-act play of star-crossed lovers,
    past the household creatures—
           the potpourri jar
exuding sweetness, the captured knight
        and the ivory castle,
    the knave of hearts
        doubling with self-love—
and I'll take you with me over the doused embers
    into the dark heart
  of the stove,
where we'll climb together towards the stars
       bracketed inside the chimney,
    past firebrick and flue
          into the stratosphere.

WONDERS OF THE DEEP

The mermaid speaks:

I suffer myself to come unto you—
                    my twinkling radiance
               hardly a star,
          but it's more than I can tell you:
                              I'm hotter than you are.
                    My fetching light
          will shine for you
                    beneath your darkest door. I'm
                         kind for you; I'm blind
               for you; I'll find you
                         o'er and o'er. *Oh,*
lead us not . . . you say, you pray, but still
                         I ask for more. Hello,
                    hello, oh no, oh no, oh yes, goodbye,

               and still I'll ask for more.
Oh, let this pass for love for me
                    for I will take allure,
          but each time that you come
                              to me I hear you say
               you cannot take no more. A
     double naught, and so we ought, and so
                    we go for more. And here's
               the room we do it in—
                              on scaling stair, on wingéd chair,
                    on top the ocean floor, and

                    swimming o'er and o'er,
            the lookdown fish will shine
for us above the conch's roar.

GRAVE WISDOM

Those of you who speak in your sleep
                    are invited, so if you choose,
        you may follow the will-o'-the-wisps
                        in a procession of torches
            to the Elf Hill ball, for only humans
                with uneasiness underlying
                    may enter the earth
            to consort with the merman
                    and his daughters, the grave
                        pig, the death horse, and the church
                lamb, and the river sprite,
                        and the goblins. Come,
    calls the nightjar, and watch the hollow maidens
                            dancing in the hallway
            with scarves of mist and moonshine,
                    but if you look too closely
                        or watch too long,
        one of them may vanish and one
                will walk beside herself
            as if she were a shadow. Come
    take the low road along the marshes,
                    where the sages' voices rise
                        like wind over the wild sloes
                as they speak on and on
                in chorus
                to the father stork

of love and its differences, of the love
of lovers, of light
for vegetation, of parents
for children—

Of the love of lovers:

It's there, you know, though
you say you want to let it go.

How does it go?

'Zackly like that—don'cha know,
don'cha know, don'cha know. . . .

You're wrong, you know, to let it go.

Of light for vegetation:

Oh, how does your garden grow,
mistress mistress?

With love and kisses
and silver belles and

the cockles of hell
and pretty maids all in a row.

Of the love of lovers:

You're wrong, you know, to let it go.

Of parents for children:

> *Of sisters for brothers,*
> *of sisters and brothers*
> *for fathers and mothers,*

Of lovers for lovers:

> *Of all the others,*
> *you're wrong, you know, to let it go.*

ON THIN ICE

Then we lifted the cans of snow
to flock the tree in our sixth grade classroom
& we sprayed the stencils
pressed against the windows
to make snowflakes, each one different,
believing, because we were told,
that under a microscope
each powdery flake of real snow
has its own composition. That's the first
I'd heard of formal variance, & I
could see that no matter
how far into the deep woods
I would go, each little particulate grief
would have a structure. It's for memory's
sake, the teacher told us,
the words are arranged by rules
of poetic composition, & in my sleep,
the rhymes kept repeating,
like our fingers drumming against the desktops
as we scanned verse, lost in reveries
that had little to do with meaning,
but rose instead from sound,
playing in the preholiday afternoons
like music. Swedenborg said the angels
express thought with consonants
that clack across the tongue
in regimental order, while feeling flows
through the vowels, small in number,

but always essential in making
a whole. My brother wrote words
backwards, as if he'd already been where
the rest of us would go. *Tell me
what it's like there*, I think
I wanted to say, cupping my mittened hands
around each syllable, but my brother
lay on the white sheet
of the hospital bed, unmoving,
like a branch in an icy field we walked
away from. Across the frozen tundra,
Gerda traveled to bring Kay home,
& when she found him at the Snow Queen's
palace, her breath froze in the air
into clouds of angels. I do not know
how long Kay struggled
under the Northern Lights to solve
the Ice Puzzle of Reason, pushing
the letters over the earth
to form *eternity*, but I know
that as long as his heart was pierced
with a fragment of evil, the work
he did was useless. Once my brother
put down the ragged pieces
of a life he couldn't fit
together. It's by sheer will
he's come back, following
the tracks across each wintry page
he holds before him, & when
he stumbles, the austere & beautiful
face of the Snow Queen
turns & mocks him at the window.

IV

AFFINITIES

Once a year in Port Meadow the grazing animals
are impounded, then returned
when statutory fines are paid by the owners.
On a conspiratorial morning the Sheriff of Oxford rides
with young women on ponies through the yellow ragwort
to corral the cows and horses.
It is an unannounced occasion, but today in the air
there is conquest, so I move carefully
through the grass, feeling collectible.
Beside me, you are adept at avoiding the plume-thistles
that choke the path, and I am sad at your skill
with physics because I believe you have
a truck with the heavens that I can never have.

"In this tomb lies Rosamond, the Rose of the World, the fair
but not the pure": Rosamond, the mistress of Henry II,
lies in Godstow Nunnery, and she seems
to have been given into our company, the frill
of her clothing brushing past as she follows us
along the path by the tea-colored water of the Isis.
By the end of the summer you will discover
that you love your wife, or will decide to, but for now
please walk slowly. . . .
It is the hint of Rosamond that tells me—
her shy, sympathetic words materializing,
though not distinctly, into the way I will move
toward each select and sinful disposition.

OXFORD, ON AN ANCIENT
CROSSROADS BESIDE
THE THAMES

We meet in the park because it is ancient
and well planned.
It feels particular,
our walk becoming part of a miniature order.
The crocuses look stemless,
set down like teacups by a careful hand,
and the footbridge is formed
in a curve of suspension.

You tell me that once black swans
imported from Australia floated on the Thames.
Because it is final,
our conversation is distilled,
comes down to objects.
Goldfish circle the ornamental pond.

I never told you that sometimes I went alone
to the Botanical Gardens,
slipping into the greenhouse
to smell the lemon scent of the foppish magnolias.
There were nights in Mississippi
so dark you could see the green hay
begin to smolder in the barn,

and the cows moved without substance
through the barbed-wire fences.

I had a treehouse,
its cypress planks scaled down, child-size,
to hold one body.
It would drift like a raft on the branches.
Though my brothers worked ropes through the trees
for sending messages,
there was sadness in their intricate system.

We have lost disorder.
I talk of the monkey-puzzle trees
that we are passing
and wallabies with insatiable appetites for roses.
You recognize it is only information,
as we become by talking.

Though we could rig up pulleys
to carry things between us,
the operation would be makeshift and small.
It is good that you are leaving.
The figure we made together has symmetry here
and will stay, provided for, on simple ground.

THE POOL OF TEARS

Life, what is it but a dream?
        —Lewis Carroll

Down the dark streets of Jericho past the Dream-glo roses
to the cups of tea steaming on the patio before us,
the fragile veins of the china and the flavor of tea
smoking through the water: the "agony of the leaf,"
they call it, the process of transforming one thing into another. . . .

This is the decline, I guess, of love into companionship,
though you say it is not clear to you how it happened.
To teach you what I know of desire, we must go indoors
and kneel before the bottom drawer of the bureau,
pulling the gold handles, and there beyond the dark veneer
and the latticework of the carved pineapples,
we'll put things away, slowly now, into the shadows.
Follow me then past the mothballs and cedar
to the watery shade of childhood, the wood wedged
against the trunks of the crepe myrtles to form a table,
Pitiful Pearl and the sock monkey waiting, incorrigibly sad,
for I did not know that the ways of love are errant,
and when I came too late, sugar spilling through the weave
of the picnic basket, they were old and bedraggled.
How suddenly it seemed to happen, the summer shower,
the overturned chairs and the tissue blossoms clinging
to the table, the clothing transparent against my body
as I dashed through the arbor to the shuttered house,
and the pool of tears, my face pressed into the pillow,
while the Planetary Winds whistled inconsolably down the chimneys.

Oh, subliminal foragings,
the flattened grasses and the rush-bottomed chairs,
and the storybook open to the creatures of dreams,
the school in the sea and the never-ending study
of Mystery and Uglification and Grief and Laughing.
When Reverend Dodgson rowed Alice Liddell and her sisters
through dull weather from Folly Bridge to Godstow,
having left behind wire puzzles and safety pins
for little girls' dresses, a thrush stirred under
Alice's breastbone, though, as the afternoon wore on,
and he turned to a tale of tumbling down a long tunnel,
she grew petulant and withdrew from the others.
He spoke then of the Hatter and the March Hare and the riddle
at the tea party of a writing desk and a raven,
for he saw that the bird inside her had grown dark and sexual.

THE COMPANY WE KEEP

Do you know we stayed two houses apart
one night without knowing, while Pickwick Dam's power
generated light in the windows
of the houses on the mountain
to make star shapes that were electrifying?
You stayed in a house with your wife,
a daughter who resembles her mother,
and a small son who misplaces his glasses
and fears and loves his older sister,
while I, together in another house
with Viston and Sheryl and Steve and Jan and Roses,
left guitars and a piano and moved
into the kitchen to make music
with measuring spoons thrummed against pots
and a collander, an eggbeater whirring,
and the door of the dishwasher closing and opening and closing.

Let's meet once at the equinox in this kitchen
to take the brown-shelled eggs from a carton
and balance them on end for thirty minutes.
You will explain that the greatest show of physics
is what we know: the way we travel in life
through multiple dimensions, or stand, as I stood once
in Houston, haunted by a small tornado
that crossed the house, flattened down the banana trees,
and opened the kitchen door and all the kitchen cabinets
to release forever a world of household spirits.

ALBUMEN AND SILVER

1

Dreamsicles swirling on a stick,
45s turning on a spindle, a De Soto
peeling off on its whitewalls. . . .

Spinning our wheels
through the dog days of August,
we spread the family photographs,
unmounted, across the table.
If we don't label these pictures,
my mother says,
they'll disappear from history.

Who's this? Oh, it's . . .
Pie and Aunt Dolly,
all shawls and fringes,
standing over the rose burners
in Heaven's kitchen,
boiling divinity
to fill your mittens.

There's Granny
skedaddling the chickens.
She fries the eggs
in the skillet
that watch you
while you're sleeping.

And here's Jinx
(our Scottish terrier)
in a toy stroller.
He's buried in an orange crate
below the garden.
He's your luck in a box;
you'll be childless.

But we leave them
unmarked,
named only in memory,
and year after year
the subjects lie there,
accusingly,
under the cracked surfaces,
until even our own bodies,
younger then, seem hardly to know us.

2

And over and over,
like an omen,
one photo emerges:
in the *Womanless Wedding*,
performed on the lawn
of Jefferson College,
my father plays the bridegroom,
wearing a shalloon-lined uniform
with intaglio buttons,
and there beside him
in the frets and bustles
of women's dresses

are all the beautiful boys.
Oh, see the bouquets
of radish tops
they carry
and all their wiggy tresses.
Between world wars,
this is the bridal party,
comic and divine.
How could my father know,
standing at the edge
of that virgin forest
in Mississippi,
that his own daughter
would marry a man
who did not want women
and that for her
forever after
fear will lie with passion?

FROZEN CHARLOTTES

Far down into the dark reaches
of human waste
and sorrow,
you go in search of Frozen Charlottes—
porcelain dolls tossed into privies
under the tupelos
by children bored
with the way they lay so still,
and now, whiter than snow,
they're lined in rows
inside your glass cabinet—moonglow, glacial,
gardenias floating all day
on silver racks
in the icebox. Sometimes they are whole,
and sometimes they're broken,
though not, I'd say, in spirit,
so stoic they look, so
disdainfully composed. I'd like
to know the secret
of these fallen women,
that I, too, could lie peacefully
beside your Flow Blue china,
having come at last
beyond defilement into luster.

Because you're my brother, I do not ask you
how you woo them, though I know
of men who find women

flagrante delicto
and lift them out of the mire
long enough to love them,
or to love themselves
for their own goodness. To the one
who loves, it hardly matters. Do
they love you back, or having been exposed,
do they turn
into themselves, pearling
forever in bewildering beauty? When
you walk along the creek meanders,
where the deer blow warning
in the understory,
do you wish sometimes for me
someone would hold me?

Smoking grapevine, you go
down the loess roads, far
into the canebrake, past the lady's slippers
and the nodding lady's tresses,
to dig into the midden
with your pick and shovel,
lowering your bucket
on a rope into the hole
to draw up trapdoor
spiders, half dimes, minié balls, and Light
Dragoon buttons, and you bring
these female dolls
into the open, turning them
in your hands over
and over—brushing
the earth from their shining
buttocks, an arm outstretched

with hand extended, their legs
pressed together so tightly
they are one limb
that cannot be parted.

DESPAIR

To you I said, can you show me
        the way we should go
            together. And you told me
of the indigo buntings, turned loose
    in the planetarium, navigating
        around Betelgeuse and Polaris,
    according to the pattern of the heavens. Now,
to me, you say nothing. And so,
        not knowing,
I wonder when you walk in alone
        under the dome of the operating theater
    to float the Swan,
            what guides you?

        You stood over me
at the hospital after my car
            was demolished
                on the driver's side,
    and the emergency equipment arrived,
            the jaws of life and the ambulance.
You said it was not Fate, but I,
            who turned the wheel
                into the intersection.
    And when I asked you what is the fluttering
        inside my organs, you said
it was only me and my ravening wonder. You told me
            the rings on my hands
        had severed the tendons. You never understood

why I wore them,
the pearls and garnets and gold
encircling my fingers
that now lie useless. In the first X-ray photograph
of the hand of the wife of Wilhelm Roentgen,
the dark shadows on the film
cast by the denser structures
show a ring she wore. Could she not bear,
even for that moment,
to have nothing to hold her?
Where are my rings? Where in the darkness
are you who rose over me? Where
are the Verities
stripped down like virgins?
Oh, bird, ring, fire in the eye,
we have no answer.

MOVING PICTURES

Because you are a doctor with silver instruments
                              to administer the ethers
that put to sleep the living so their bodies can be opened,
you surprise me by looking lost among the leaf rot
                  and moon vine in a ravine near the Mississippi River—
you, a New Yorker, with a Nikon camera and telephoto lens
                                        to draw things closer.
You will show slides with a projector that lights the sky bluer
              and things we can hardly know will look more possible
                              than they ought to.

When my brothers and I were children out under the stars
                              in lawn chairs folded open
beside the door of the paneled station wagon, we ate popcorn slowly,
watching men and women larger than the oak trees
                        beside the screen of the drive-in cinema,
while the cidadas vibrated their timbals
                  through the double feature in a kind of fusion.

We grow up smaller than glamour—you and I, our dramas domestic
                        and boxed small enough for television,
David and Ginger coming home from a party after arguing mildly
to find the television had been struck by lightning,
                              its mechanism welded
so they couldn't turn it off, and on the screen the people were lost
                  in snow that seemed to go on forever.

Ahead of me, you raise your camera to take a picture
of a railway car that someone lives in,
its strip of windows trimmed in silver.
In movies, trains race across continents, while people sleep in berths,
at speeds so great the wheels turn backwards.
You, who have come to me from a vast distance,
can hardly believe that someone lives on the Southern Pacific
in a passenger car, uncoupled.

PEONIES

Drifting on the downside of love, when all
must be retrieved, brought home again,
I see myself standing at the end
of the path in my childhood—the sky
above me darkening—& I am holding
a little pail & shovel,
frightened, I think, because it's later
than it should be, so I must whistle
softly with bravado to hear myself,
so far down the path I look
smaller than I ought to, while you looking out
on my room we made love in
are finding it even harder to fetch yourself,
so lost you look in this bower
you call "so brutally feminine,"
now that we are drawn apart on the other side
of ardor; thus it is I must take your hand
to lead you out past the fluted lamps,
past the scrolled cage suspended
from the ceiling—the artificial cardinal
on the red swing swinging, past the Sirens
bending over—their tendrilous locks flowing
over the ovolo moulding, their rosebud
mouths open, open, singing. . . . Then you & I
go hand-in-hand into the parlor
to the vase that holds a whole flock
of fluffed-up peonies, looking
as if they have walked to the edge of water

to dip their beaks in, their sickles
& saddle feathers spread wide
for bathing. Once a year, at least,
I must have them—too big, I'd say,
for beauty. If you could know me truly,
you could hide with me there
in the tangled vine at the end of the path,
two doors down from my grandmother's
house, where the hens fly loose
from the broody coop, their rose combs
quivering, & the rooster bobs
his crested head, a *miles gloriosus*
patrolling along the paling,
guardian of this grassy lot & the dark bordering
alley. Then out on the stoop come
the aging spinsters—glowering sibyls
who point us children towards the gates
of hell, promising us
we'll get there. Old maids, old maids,
can't get a husband, the neighborhood boys
call back, their voices rising
from the hollow, & though the day has barely
broken, the sisters cross the yard
to wring the necks of the waiting chickens,
their feathers ruffled
like these blossoms on the edge
of dying. Headless, they rise to go up
the porch steps & back down again,
their bodies remembering what their tiny brains
no longer tell them. . . . & in the gathering
light, I throw down my bucket
& its hoard of eggs some stray hen laid,

filched from the shadows—one
with a window a baby chick pipped open—
lost forever; though later, to console me,
Mama & Aunt Gay will take me
down the block to Robinson's Drugstore
to drink floats with the workers
from the hosiery mill at the table
where John Scopes sat down to argue
for teaching the origin of man, & I'm
glad, I say, I came from a monkey,
so little *I've* seen of the floss & gold
of the angels they tell me
peer down on us from the heavens. I spend
my pennies on Atomic Fireballs & a glass ring,
its band expandable. Who, then, they ask,
laughing, will you marry? . . . *No one, no one,*
& in the late afternoon the chimes
from Bryan Hill drifting over the valley,
Mama will sit before the vanity
in the one upstairs bedroom,
the oscillating fan blowing, to take
off the face she "puts on" each morning,
the jar of vanishing cream open on the table,
while I, outside with the other children,
slip the skins off the scuppernongs
& place them in a petri dish,
shallow enough for feeling, & line up
sun-dried apricots & pasta swirling
in a bowl, taking each thing one by one,
blindfolded, believing, naming
the parts—eyeballs, ears,
the working brain—

willing ourselves to touch them,
even with our tongues, these human parts,
our hearts in our throats, our bodies
shivering, partly afraid, partly ecstatic.